Rebirth of Venus

Jacqui Lalita

Pachamama Publishing
ISBN 978-0615509372

For Mimes and Mama J

Special Thanks

Cover design by Danielle Avila Johnston
www.omsites.com

Cover photo by Leelu Morris
www.leelumorris.com

Back cover photo by Theron Nelson

Thank you to the precious trees who offered their skins for these pages to turn.

To the millions of sensitive, wild animals
of our world in captivity ~
To the fox on fur farms, pigs in slaughterhouses,
elephants under the bullhook of circuses,
dogs on chains passing their days alone:
May your limbs know freedom, your heart taste peace,
your paws and hooves hold hands
with the millions of humans who care about you,
praying for change.

Contents

Straight from the light-infused darkness of ecstatic galaxies comes this humble hearth of poetry. From the honeysuckle Holiness within that drips from my lips in this time of the great turning, I offer you all my yearning and burning and the many ways I sing praise to spellbound days that never cease to amaze. Moon swoon play me a tune, intoxicate me with jasmine's bloom. Truth or chance, the spontaneous dance of whimsical winds upon my spine.

How the Heavens circled for us this precise moment in time!

Here comes dawn, passion spawned, lovers tender as a newborn fawn. Now we rise with the aurora in our eyes, arms extended to life's sweet surprise, bowing to the days, nights and secret spaces in between.

Sweet Life ~ Maiden of Mystery ~
we are your children, lovers, kings and queens.

Creatress

Primordial creation of vines and veins
sweet rains who became rivers rushing
into the great blue deep

Steep in the immortal elixir of life who brews
with clues of her essence in all places
traces of the traceless
faces of the faceless
impeccable beauty
whose name remains nameless

Everything connected to every thing.
Sing aloud as a nightingale to the throbbing night

Moonlight shines upon all souls alike.

Many hues of the great muse
her flowers, herbs and trees stirring
midnight reveries, messages on the wings
of migratory birds

Words channeled through umbilical cords
swords cutting through the chains that bind
A mind set free
amidst a blaze of alchemy

She is our mother line to the divine
Creatress of abounding glory
whose story and myth spills across the Earth
the rebirth of Venus

Sacred feminine returning
Burning in the bellies of every woman alive

Dive deeply into the source of joy within
Spin naked under the full moon

Inhale…exhale…a burgeoning breath
of widening scope

Hope is a thing with wings.

Becoming the Butterfly

We seek pleasure and avoid pain,
plunge towards happiness and thwart grief

but what rainbow ever filled the sky with its beauty
without a rain storm first?

What bold heart ever opened to offer the best of itself
without first tasting the ancient ache of loss?

You rest in a chrysalis of transformation
where deep within the chambers of your ailing heart
destined rapid change is underway
Even in your pain, can you sense
the imminent emergence of new wings?

Flashes of Love

Some come like lightning

Flashes of fierce love to electrify the night
bursting at the seam with joy,
overflowing with a love so perfect and pure

Some come like thunder
crashes of passion rumbling across this fragile life
helping us remember the power and potency
inside each moment

Some come like rain
showering our lives with a happiness
we didn't know we thirsted for,
drenching our souls in joy
quenching our hearts with love
each time we see them
smiling

Some linger like rainbows
streaking their memory across eternity,
painting the sky with a beauty so brilliant,
a life so boldly lived,
one can only tip their heads up and believe...

There is a passageway to Infinity
for souls like this
who blast our tender hearts wide open,
who fill our days with magic and laughter
who teach us the beautiful and difficult lessons
of loving and letting go

For the ones who come and go too quickly,

We shall find you again and again
in the lightning, in the thunder,
in every blade of grass
And again in every flower, moon and wild streak of sun
Go now back to the Infinite
We shall find you in the One.

Un-contacted Tribes

Earthquakes of unprecedented magnitude,
tsunamis pummeling the lands,
nuclear meltdowns and oil stained seas

I cannot find the poetry in suffering
nor smell the peonies and pristine old growth forests
when our planet is turning herself inside out

But find solace in knowing that somewhere right now,
as reactors explode and senseless wars ensue,
there are un-contacted tribes deep within the Amazon
who have never seen a plane nor tasted a Coca Cola.

Somewhere right now, there are people
cooking grains over the fire
under ancient constellations of stars

Sharing stories that were their grandparents stories,
who have no word in their whole language for "nuclear"
and even some, I imagine, who have no word for war.

Wild Woman Creation Story

In a time outside of time before the dawn of Adam and Eve
the spirit of Wild Woman was immaculately conceived

Galactic gyrations and spirals of light
gave Wild Woman the gift of flight

She came as crashing thunder pouring down the rain
and the Universe for this moment would never be the same

Wild Woman parted her lips to sing and gave the birds
their destined wings
Wild Woman shook her hips to dance
and colored the world in a state of trance
The winds began to roll, the wolves began to howl
and there upon her shoulder sat all-seeing totem owl

From bursting girth she gave birth to Earth
From her third eye came the sky
Such joy the birds had found their home inspired her to cry

She stirred her tears into a passionate potion
that soon became wide open ocean
With outstretched arms she began to whirl
and the spirit of dolphins came unfurled
Wild woman spread her legs
laying embryos and crystal eggs
stones and bones, gushing rivers, vital livers
She shivered all the world alive amidst orgasmic quivers

The spirit of Shiva and Shakti simultaneously revealed
lush gardens exploding with fruits waiting to be un-peeled

Wild Woman dreamed a mighty lion to guide the way
to the land of Zion
She planted fields of corn and rice
seeding ripe paradise

She was maiden, mother and wise old crone
who contained all mysteries to the great unknown

She came as crashing thunder before the dawn of time
delivering the holy word
in spellbound lyric rhyme

In a flash of light Wild Woman appeared
to set this Universe free
then she hid herself in the deepest depths
inside you and me.

Hereafter

I watched your silver hair turning white
as dusk gave way to night
the beautiful form you were, at once returned to light

Here, after all these years
climbing mountains of hope
swimming rivers of tears

Here, after all this time on Earth
entwined in delicate webs
life, death, rebirth

Our initiation through transformation
Our invocation to illumination
What other realms await behind that sacred gate?
What seas have we to sail with the parting of the veil?

To live each moment fully awake
embracing the Great Unknown
Death finds each one of us alas,
we shall not go alone

What worlds reside on the other side?
what impenetrable mysteries have we to cross?

I hear the sound of your laughter everywhere now
and know there is no true loss

The hereafter is not so far
and we, descendants of the stars
like all kin shed old skin
to move through portals
when the veils are thin

Our immortal souls eternal
your transition I shall not mourn
but celebrate your great awakening
in the light of life we are reborn.

We Are the Dancers

Dancing
we are those who weave
Heaven and Earth in infinite figure eights
We are living prayers spinning a wisdom of ages
with a soft web of innocence

We are hot rhythm of blood
sultry melody of steaming lips.
Story tellers and muses who desire
only to inspire rippling chills up your spine
as you witness the dance
and leave your seat believing

We are those who seek immortality
And so we dance
For when we are bending our bodies
towards Earth and Sky
leaping through air,
whirling within ancient spirals,
undulating from the depths of our core,
shaking hips wildly loose and hearts wide open,

It is then that we know we are going to live forever.

Love Liberated

I was dwelling in my highest dreams
barreling the ocean's wave
when all at once it dawned on me
I had nothing left to save.

Every tiny piece of me I offered to the sea
Oh Mother of All please take from me
that which is not free!

Strip me of attachment
Quell my incessant desire
Hold me under water
Purify me in your fire

Oh let me be the great observer
witnessing the tides fall and rise
Let me carry the healing medicine wheel
in the rings within my eyes
Let my journey be an ancient labyrinth
through the garden of creation
Let my being be a blooming flower oozing inspiration!

I was on my knees inside that wave
dwelling in my highest dreams
when all at once it dawned on me
life is not always what it seems

We are so much more than we may know
we are wind and root and seed
and deep within these sacred forms
resides everything we ever need

We are wild artichokes
with many layers there to peel
and a heart of succulent perfection waiting to be revealed

We are soul and spine together
we are serpent, we are hawk,
we are cosmos, we are soil,
to fly we must first walk.

We are the rooted reach
the humble steps inside of flying
the supreme breath of the present moment
the living inside of dying

Oh show me love liberated!
I sang out to the sea
and there it was revealed to me

We are everything.
We are free.

Heirs to Infinity

We were gods once and we knew it.
And once upon a choice we danced
to the rhythm of our soul
moved by the whims of wind
broken open by late night piercings of lightning
blown on weeping clouds

into caverns that dripped with delicate longing
where star seeds
blossomed in secrecy
within slippery wombs
and chaos gave birth
to a simple life

Once upon a choice
we became fire and were no longer burned by it.
We changed. Everything changed.

Under a crimson sky life became a theater
where only the loving took front row.
By night the moon grew legs and danced
inside the dark corners of our hearts.

Within the rising tides we found
an amulet of abundance,
a talisman of trust
and a gleaming gem of generosity

Upon this golden Earth
we were melted by the hot ooze of molten rock
silenced by the godliness of deer,
rendered still by the majesty of mountains

Once upon a choice
we were creation and creator

A strong people given mostly to dancing
under crimson skies
with bodies made of water
who thirsted for the good word
to sing and sing again:

We are the heirs to infinity.

A Wild One

I was a wild one once`

When I think about those death-defying antics of old,
the perceived invincibility with which I pushed the limits
regularly burning the candle at both ends,
I feel utterly grateful to have arrived in this garden
with a cup of tulsi tea and the lapping waves at my toes.

There are many crazy moments I could have died,
zipping around highways on the wrong side
with that blind cab driver in Egypt
or being kidnapped from a dark street in the capital of Peru
from a man desperately pleading for marriage

and saner ways too I nearly died,
dangling from the mountain's edge
in moments of passionate romance

But still and at long last...
I am here,
truly here
sensing the precious, fleeting gift of this flesh
no longer burning to taste near death experience

but to taste near life!

Those moments of soul-tingling revelry
when the garden of creation hums
through every blossoming, crawling,
flying, and waking being,
When the sight of my ten vibrant fingers

and the ancient lines across my palms
that only I bear
sends me rushing towards that tremendous edge
dangling in ecstatic disbelief
that it could all be true.

I was a wild one once
dodging death and pushing the limits
until one mystic night I came face to face
with my own wild, untamed soul
tasting the wine of liberation, and knowing
there would be no turning back.

Twilight Nectar

Running at dusk is salve for the soul
nature is medicine so untold

Passions, pleasures, worries and woes
disappear on those trails right under my nose
a chorus of crickets, a grand orchestra of birds
a silent heart that needs no words

There were responsibilities, goals, intentions, ambition
unfinished projects awaiting fruition
yearnings and dreams for what might one day be
the world's distress aching in me

Then there was nothing
but twilight's embrace
with that familiar, cunning tickle of grace
seductive Venus lighting the night
and a deep inner knowing this life was just right

That somehow destiny had woven her hand
to deliver me whole to this medicine land
There was a song in my soul that only dusk knew
a calling to merge with all that is true

There was this moment, this breath, this life, this now
what else could I do but bow?
Untold are the ways that nature heals
profound are the lessons she reveals
take a walk with the moon, rise for the dawn
marvel at her wisdom spawned

The soul song sings when mind is calm
by way of twilight's healing balm
and clarity gives a golden key
unlocking the greatness we can be

Goodbye to yesterday and all future plans
I've arrived at church on medicine lands

Nature is the perfect place to pray
Silence a most holy thing to say.

Sleeping Lady Awakens

Let me take you to a world
where nature reigns supreme
where everything exists inside a dream within a dream

Sleeping lady is awakening to fly on verdant wings
to rouse the owl nation with the blood songs that she sings

The spell of the sensuous shall return once more
utters the Oracle through cryptic moans
and we can feel hot marrow stirring deep within our bones

The air is thick with moss, the ground is laden in dew
Now we find ourselves crossing a bridge
between the old world and the new

We touch our toes upon the new
and become drenched in violet flowers
as third eyes ignite the sight of psychic intuitive powers
all beings appear as light and there exists no separation
and all at once we are rising to meet this higher vibration

All creatures are free now, enslavement has disappeared
the wind and sun fuel us and sacred water is revered
Soul mates find each other here
and polarities become complete
and under full moons we go dancing naked with bare feet

The lands are lush between our toes
replete with bursting seeds
and everyone from all cultures fulfills their heartfelt needs

Art and love are being made
creativity is a way of life

One can overturn each rock and pebble but find no hint of strife
Harmony takes root as our old stories are cleared
and love comes to fill the spaces of all that we once feared

We are praying together now
All are One, so shall it be!
Alas we are crossing this bridge of Earth's great destiny

The golden eagle is illuminating pathways once unknown
and hand in hand alas are finding our way home

Sleeping Lady is awakening, the owl nation is taking flight
and from the ashes we are rising to regain our primal sight

The spell of sensuality drips from every leaf and tree
and from our third eyes lotus flowers bloom
I see you… Do you see me?

Spring Serenade

This morning over roasted dandelion tea
spring wrapped herself around us on a patch of paradise
where a million creatures danced together
to the chorus of blue jays and humming birds

Lavender flowers opened themselves for bees to pollinate
butterflies fluttered their beauty to and fro
lady bugs climbed up blades of grass
and that wild day star shined majesty upon us all
nourishing plants, tanning skins, warming Earth
and the hearts of all Earthlings with the light of 1000 rays

Looking out over the rolling green hills of Topanga
I imagined all the little communities of creatures
on patches of grass like ours, seen and unseen,
doing their work to make this spring day so beautiful,
offering all of their life force to keep these mountains so alive.

I hope wherever you are, whoever you are,
your work somehow contributes to the harmony
of the greater whole, that somehow you rise
each day to offer the best of yourself
to keep this world humming with beauty

and that on mornings like this, or silent evenings too,
amidst the revelry of spring
you sip your tea and marvel
at your special place in it all.

True Love

What depths of pure love I have known
what tender whispers have wrapped themselves
around my heart have come and gone
washed out in the rains
that tap like a ghost tonight
upon my window

I have tasted loneliness in the clutches
in some of the world's most stunning men
felt their perfect forms pressing down on me
like a prison I yearned to escape from under

I have charmed and been charmed
by the most captivating among them
He whose moonlit serenades and fits of passion
have wilted me by dawn
He whose long line of admirers
has winced in envy as we kissed

He is coming to my window now
with smooth song and velvet wine
a kind word and a sly eye

But the rains are tumbling down
blurring his great beauty
and at last, it is the soul I wish to stroke

For I have tasted true love
held it against my bones
inhaled its exquisite scent
danced inside its majestic corridors

and for this,
there are no lips so intriguing
no moonlit serenade
nor vintage cabernet

that can call my attention away from the rains
that tap like a ghost upon my window
carrying memories of that which was
for a fleeting moment in time,
a beacon of all that is possible.

Love Is

Passion on the rocks
    summer nights kissing to Otis Redding
        while sitting on the docks

A fine wine of honey laced with inspiration
    a merging of two souls
        from the heights of source creation

Love is
    a gentle river flowing to the sea
        A mingling of two breaths fulfilling destiny
            First flight of hummingbird set free from its cage
                Sweet smoke of palo santo coalescing with white sage

Cherry blossoms in full bloom,
    sips of hot spiced chai
        Moonlight on the water, ancestral starlight in the sky
            The deepest of all depths traversing the highest heights
                microcosmic orbits exploding in delights

Love is
    a window to our souls
        an expansive doorway of perception
            A temple of sacred mirrors reflecting divine perfection

Forgiveness and acceptance
    a radical stripping away of fears
        the welcomed dance of surrender in laughter-coated tears

Love is
    late nights by the firelight
        early mornings by the stream
            Bodies throbbing to unheard melodies
                piercing through the dream

Moon drenched mineral baths,
    enlivening alpine trees
        nature's healing pulse
            that brings us to our knees

An ancient medicine flute resounding
    across the dawn
        Love is the most purifying
            song among all songs.

The Belly Dancer

*"Most poets are like a belly dancer who never reveals anything
below her waist." ~Rumi*

Belly dancer, poet, sensuous weaver of the seen and unseen
with keen mind and honeyed hips
whose lips curl and smile as if holding a secret key

~ Destiny~
finds us wherever we turn

with words that burn to explode across the page
she is sparking sage and frankincense
ancient scents, an inner sense
of peace

Release the chains that bind one's mind
innocence reveals what silken clothes conceal
a shoulder roll, a demure glance
suspended now within her dance

Ancient hieroglyphics coursing
through her veins
healing rains come pouring down
as she roams from town to town
and many a man drops to his knees
when she undulates beneath the trees
with spontaneous prose
nobody knows what gentle powers she holds in hand
nor can they fathom
or dare to imagine
where or when she'll land.

Good News

Attention kings and queens, royalty of Earth's high court
I come to you today with good news to report!
It blows in on the winds of change and sings of transformation
reminding us all beings are all from one great nation

The messengers have sent their words on the white wings of a dove
that the ruling party ever-more shall be the power of love
and all beings shall be liberated and all hearts set forever free
This is the moment we have long awaited in ancient prophecy

The feminine is re-emerging to share her gentle ways
Great Goddess Mother of All, here us sing your praise!
Wise plant teachers are coming forth to be our gentle guide
that we may walk this path with courage
and compassion at our side

Ascended Masters are speaking, Archangels are offering clues
Heaven on Earth exists right now, it is up to us to choose
If we choose selfless love and service to each other
and the great Divine
I can say with such conviction, we are going to be just fine

Our souls will heal, as will this land
In perfect timing with the master plan
And so all kings and queens, gods and goddesses... that means YOU
the messengers have said there is just one thing we must do
There in vivid color on the white wings of a dove
was the answer to it all:

Love, Love, Love, Love, Love!

Gypsy Woman

Gypsy woman sleeps outdoors to be close to the wild call
of coyote and crow
who remind her to always

hold hands with freedom.
By night, pure molecules of air
laden with stardust blanket her dreams

She spins tin cans of trust into
golden opportunity
light and dark into
effervescent rainbows of inspiration,
passion and purpose adorn each adventure
to beckon her imagination

She is a wisdom seeker in flowing skirt
and a pocket full of intuition
that carries her across landscapes and cultures,
down rivers and up mountains,
with tambourine on one hip and trust on another

She is a close friend of plant kin, an ally of ancient ways
dancing naked under full moons
whole and holy across the days

She makes love at any hour and brews her magic in the night
and with bare feet she goes spinning
earthly breath into rays of light!

Gypsy woman! Gypsy woman! Powerful is your stance!
Riding the tails of comets with a body made to dance!
Gypsy woman! Gypsy woman! Glorious are your wings!
Riding the crest of waves with a soul that forever sings!
You twirl your dress as you spin and the Gods come closer to peek
Oh Gypsy Woman, you are the freedom
each soul silently seeks

Lover of life, wandering wayfarer,
fragrant gypsy moving to the beat of tambourines,
at home you are in the forest, dreaming in the desert,
visioning by the sea, wild hair flowing on the breeze,
your heart is ever-free!

Moving from village to village naked as the moon,
skin glistening in the sun,
some raise their eyebrows as you pass
Beautiful woman come undone!

Your caravan is the Beloved, your tribe spreads far and wide,
there is magic where you are
down double rainbows how you slide!

Go now to the shores of Avalon or the mountain's mystic heights
loving every fearless moment, night by starry night!

Drumbeats!

Tambores! Flamenco in this soul!
Gypsy in this heart! Rumba in this piping blood!
Tango in these passionate thighs pleading
to wrap themselves around this world alive!

Tambores! Drums beating, rattles shaking,
Sufi whirling down a double helix road
to the unfathomable mysteries of old!

There are notes in between the rhythms,
portals in between each breath,
a narrow edge meant to be ridden,
straddling life and death.

In the dawn when the light takes hold,
a new chance to start afresh
Oh Tambores, Tambores, Tambores!
Take this swollen heart and steaming flesh!

Bathe me in trance rhythms, shake rattles across my spine
the aurora is rousing serpents in me

Long have we circled the great Divine!

Music is holy medicine the living nectar
on which I thrive, passion gushing
through my limbs pleading to wrap themselves
around this world alive!

Grace of Fire

There comes a moment in our lives
when we are asked to start over

when the cauldron of transformation sets fire to all that we know
in hopes that our soul may grow.

And so the day arrives when our timber house tumbles down
our explosive relationship combusts right before our eyes
our singeing eyebrows send us plunging into the nearest river

where we encounter the reflection of our true self
who has been patiently waiting on the wings.

There in those cool, crystalline waters we begin to see
how our soul, so long-held in abeyance,
became the arsonist for the grace of fire to burn.

And as the old walls that held our life together
crumble down, the flesh and bones
of our own wildness remain

Now for the first time in a long time
we recall the wonder we had as a child
when the Mystery was not so far away

And though thick smoke billows in every direction,
we feel our lungs able to breathe in a way
they have not for so long,
deep breaths full of vital possibility,

inspiring us to throw our arms up to the sky
and dance naked in ashes
to the aria of birdsong all around

Finally understanding what it is that makes them sing.

Broken Open

You have loved each other deeply
you have hurt each other repeatedly
you have contracted and expanded

soared the heights, plunged the depths
been the mirror and the shadow,
the inspiration and the muse

What is there to lose now
when innocence is gone
and long mornings in love's embrace
have faded into hurried farewells?

You have touched each others soul
stroked each others heart
been burned by each other
and branded in a way that will leave you
somehow never the same

You have shared moonlit magic and firelight
opens roads of untold passion
delirious laughter, desirous loins,
chocolate kisses and childhood tales
You have placed your hands on each others hearts,
looked into the infinity of each others eyes
and in that moment known.

What is left now when broken hearts have cracked open
to something beyond the pain

When nostalgia is colored in shades of melancholy
and flames of love rest
on the embers of yesterday's dreams

You have loved each other.
You have hurt each other.
Both remain, but only one is real.

When mountains of trust and rivers of hope
begin to crumble and you stand there
in the tumbling avalanche of lost majesty
feel the way an evaporating river forms a cloud
to shower sweet waters upon your dusty limbs . . .
The way a broken heart can make you whole again.

You have loved deeply.
It has come and it has gone.

This loving and letting go,
we cannot escape either of them.
They hunt us in the night
and capture us in the day
to ensure we each leave this world
with hearts broken wide open.

Betting it all on Love

Some say love is a journey of hope and sacrifice
some say it takes us years to master
some shout their bad advice

Some say all love is doomed to end
that we should beware with fragile hearts
some say love is a gamble
an elusive game of darts

Some say that only a lucky few
actually hit that bulls-eye mark
some wander through the months and years
chasing shadows in the dark

Some say to love is to suffer
heartbreak a bitter pain
some say to truly fall in love
drives the best of us insane

Some say love is not for the weary
but for the wild and the brave
some say in the purifying fire of love
one has nothing left to save

Some say the fire burns away
everything that love is not
guiding us to the sunlit path
to the bulls-eye's sacred spot

Some say that love is a journey
where the tender heart may break
I say each moment spent in love
shall be worth the exquisite ache

And so I'm betting it all on love
every penny to my name
what better way to live this life
than to gamble on love's game!

With the Current

"The time for the lone wolf is over. Gather yourselves! Banish the word struggle from your attitude and your vocabulary. All that we do now must be done in a sacred manner and in celebration. We are the ones we've been waiting for." ~ Hopi elder

And so they gathered in their communities
planted gardens, painted murals, shared magical meals
and song together by the firelight
And they jumped into the rivers across holy hours
stole kisses across sacred seconds
made every moment cause for celebration

And so it was
that Earth lit up like this
garden by community garden
Seed by seed, soul by soul
each one offering the fullness of their being
for the collective bounty to bloom

And the Sufi poet, the Hopi elder, the Nepalese monk,
the Celtic goddess dancing at the gates of Avalon
all shared what they knew of a way inward
through the vast stardust of eternities
to the center of a mustard seed
where all that was broken could be mended
and all that was hidden could be delicately revealed
And they sang from the noble silence
And they kissed the Earth with their feet
And love's effluence flowed out in all directions

to all beings, so that whichever way one turned
the air was perfumed with blossoms
and the current was there to carry them.

Moon Dancer

I'm your moon dancer, romancer, midnight entrancer
with swiveling hips that carry the answer,
to ancient mysteries and worlds unknown
transcendent are my subtle moans

That swollen moon begins to rise
now I'm mesmerized, hypnotized
with open eyes, ecstatic sighs,
moon dew dripping in between my thighs

I pierce the veil on a slow exhale,
revealing golden holy grail
this love soaked breath,
this kiss of death
dancing until there is nothing left

Music, music, everything is music!
Melodies and rhythms, orchestras of reeds
dancing to the lunar light for all the hearts that bleed

Mama Luna! Luna Bella! Gracias por tu luz!
Mother Moon! Beautiful Moon! Thank you for your light!

You inspire and delight
impel me to take flight
cast a brilliant radiance
that all at once ignites
fireworks of passion exploding in my being
truth abound all around, magnificence I'm seeing

Your grandeur spills across my face
bathed in grace, your sacred taste,
spiraling in me through the depths of space
chasing rainbows, embracing fates
the moonlit path is ever great

So I come to face the moonlit sky
dancing until the day I die
with rhyme and reason, across all seasons

Offering up my limbs to you,
moon dancing, romancing, midnight entrancing,
legs drippings with your lunar dew.

Swollen Moon Medicine

Oh Mother Moon, great guardian and muse
of mystic nights as these
Some say they are too busy to tip a head up
in revelry of your swollen grandeur,
while I remain here awe-struck again and again
at the many ways you illuminate our world

I dance beneath you tasting ancient longing
for that which has no name
A wounded heart offered to you is made whole again,
a primal desire replenished,
a thunderous throbbing for new passion and creation
ignited beneath my moonstruck skin

How you shine upon us all,
revelers and unwitting alike
I pray that my love and light upon this world
be so unconditional as yours.

Ode to the Plant Kin

There are living herbs here to help us
in profound and potent ways
some to help us grow stronger in our will
others to help us grow stronger in our hearts
some to calm our nerves
and others to enhance our minds

Nettles to nourish
Tulsi to tonify
Dandelion to detox
Parsley root to purify

Milk thistle who loves our livers
Wild cherry bark who cherishes our lungs
Ginger who soothes our bellies
Juniper berry who mends our joints

Oh where to begin sacred plant kin!
Healing roots and medicinal leaves
I find my pharmacy in the doctors of trees

Wild berries and jungle vines
delivering a higher state of mind

Living libraries of mycelial spores
unlocks perception's hidden doors

Chanterelle mushrooms after the rains
chase away winter pains

Renewal blooms from the tiniest seed
A remedy for nearly every need

Soak in the mugwort, brew your healing teas
place your trust in the wise old doctors of trees!

Wild Child

Stay wild child, take risks, be bold,
worry not of growing old
for as those wrinkles etch from days gone by
remember you will never die

Eternal spirit, ever free
Infinity your destiny
Shine and sing, howl and dance,
this moment our most precious chance
For though we shall live on forever
never will there be this day again
so say not "one day maybe when..."

This moment here so ripe and ready
and the winds of change are blowing steady
so how bout we just fly a kite
let go of such mighty might
and lay down by a holy stream
dream ourselves a little dream
or a dream so big it shakes the ground
till all around this sacred sound
Creation's song, abounding glory
resounding through our human story

Oh eyes that have beheld Thy grace
turn to face your sisters, brothers,
fathers, mothers, divine lovers
All walks, all creeds are welcome here
in this caravan there lives no fear

Surrender all your woes and pains
till the simple truth of love remains
stay wild child, kiss the sky
remember you will never die

No to GMO

They wish to control our food supply
and our minds,
to sublimate our most instinctual ways of living
so that we may follow the rancid ranks
who rise each day with some unspoken need
to conquer and control

Who knows what drives them
or what thoughts rush over them as they step outside
oblivious to the fruit trees or the watching eagle
whose eye leaps from every dollar bill

Tell me, you in stiff suit and stiffer mind,
can you fathom the meaning of eagle medicine
or why Sitting Bull wore that feather?

Can you fathom the true power of the pyramid
on the dollars bills you use to pillage this Earth
or has the smoke of illusion choked you,
the genetically modified, artificial preserved toxic
ways in which you walk upon our Mother
left you too constipated to think straight?

Hills of Belonging

On the trails
where I roam
there are no trees who are lost
nor any hawks in the sky
who do not know
their way home.

There are no foraging squirrels
dashing by who are lost,
nor any honey bees who do not know
where their queen resides.

In these woods, for a moment,
I am home.

No longer the torn woman
who set out this morning
searching for a better part of herself,

But a silent observer
of the awe-filled nature of things
tasting glimpses through fog and mist
of her inextricable place in it all.

Are humans the only creatures
who get so lost,
so sad or numbed by circumstances,
so reluctant to open themselves to life?

There are many questions
unanswered in my life today,
unknown paths ahead
where courage and conviction
must guide each step.

There is a wise, rooted woman
taking the hand of a tender inner child
and roaming through a forest
full of silent, brave creatures
who for a moment remind her
what it feels like to belong.

Soulmate

We straddled the night birthing love storm
dissolving to pure light beyond all form

I became a mermaid, you became my ocean
spirit waters flowed mightily from the seeds
of our devotion

I became a comet, you became my sky
unraveling our story in love-struck eyes

We chased each other in an electrical dance
drifting out of our bodies and into deep trance

We sipped in sunlight, bathed in blue lagoons
made love that dripped infinity under the spell of many moons

The rains came tumbling down, hearts came bursting
free as we breathed into each other inhaling destiny.

Once upon a time
we were particles of light spiraling across infinity
we were tiny seeds of creation exploding into possibility
we were algae dancing in a green forest of kelp
we were golden butterflies and you saved my life
when I needed help
we were condors of the Amazon in flight on majestic wings
we were hawks and I can still hear
the medicine songs we used to sing

We have danced together before
now again in sensuous steaming flesh
soft skins and lips coalesce
as ancient fires mesh

Sweet breath of mystic lover
breathe your mystery into me
dance inside my waterfall until the mighty waters
come gushing free

Passionate are our kisses
deep are our winding rivers
lifetime upon lifetime your touch has made me quiver

I remember we were particles of light passing by
and that lifetime when we were fireflies flashing across the sky

I remember the moment we first stepped from ocean worlds
onto sun-kissed sands
and the time when we were wild horses
galloping freely across the lands

Wrap your flesh around me
intertwine your legs with mine
incarnation after incarnation
you have been a lover most divine.

Open Road

Find me on the open road
where the river weaves through mountain bends
and my best friend's ears flop on the breeze

Where the path of grace and ease
solid ground beneath my feet
is towering enough a feat
and the midday kiss of golden rays
sets a wild heart ablaze
Where oceans rise to meet the sky
and the truth of who we are can never die

Ancient roadmaps across starry nights
shall lead you far from city lights
and the holy scriptures etched on every leaf
can remind even the most afraid part of yourself
you are powerful beyond belief

Find me on the open road
where courage trumps and freedom reigns
where dull pains fade to pleasure
and even the most heartbroken part of yourself remembers
you are loved beyond all measure

Trade your history for destiny
your old stories for untold glories
where wonder reigns in wagging tails
and unbound love indeed prevails.

Training Days

What if our most challenging moments
were meant to be training days
rather than complaining days?

What if instead of being overwhelmed by circumstance
we could dance in the wrings of fire
Inspire those around us with clarity of heart
Start a revolution with picket signs proclaiming
"Know Thyself or Bust"
What if in hard times we could learn to truly trust
Turn our bodies towards the trees and the mysteries
they hold, be bold and connected with starlight in our eyes
and a lion's heart roaring:
Live through me and dare not compromise!

What if we drank daily from the wellsprings of our passion
Sipped the nectar of compassion for ourselves and others,
Oh my sisters and brothers!
What if we were broken-open by the ocean spray,
Awed by the procession of stars
Struck by the quiet slipping in of our soul who knows
and knows again,
We are children of light

Oh the glory of sight and sound
the way love abounds in all places
leaving traces of truth for us to find

What if our minds remained calm
and instead of complaining on those fated days of training
when we are called upon to rise
Through it all we could stand up tall
carrying starlight in our eyes.

Holy Breath of Now

To be a dancer is to know
the winding corridors of bone and flesh,
the exquisite curves and outer edges of reach,
to move inside secret places of the soul
to stir and be stirred by the great song that is life

To be a dancer is to move across lineages and cultures,
to fuse ancient tradition
with the holy breath of now

To be penetrated by rhythm, melted by melody
merging with music to become at once
everything that is and ever has been

Until there is nothing left
but these bursting bones and flesh
turning across the night
to weave our stories
into some glorious fleeting sight.

We Are Getting Closer

It is ok to fall down today.
To rise with the aurora.
To surrender to the rain
and the pain that must wash over
our lives from time to time,

to trust in the revolutions and revelations
that keep us marching forth
in the blue winds that tear off our robes
and leave us shivering in the naked truth.

Through portals of time-space we are all together
weavers of one destiny
Shamans.
Sages.
Priestesses.
Pathfinders.
Dream Makers.
Wisdom Keepers.

With moonlit secrets and ancient etchings coloring our skins
We are the sweat of stars. blood of fire.
the green stalks of imagination.
We are soft tender animals simply yearning
to nourish and be nourished.

We are dancers on the crucible of transformation,
voyagers sent out into the world who sometimes
must turn the journey inward towards the soul.
Keep your arms open today. We are getting closer.

One

Look how the wind blows
how we have all arrived here
    from somewhere

Look how the story of being separate
has circulated far and wide

Each day clues arrive on the wind
    of origin and destiny,
a blue dragonfly from ancient times,
an owl feather on our doorstep,
a long gaze into the eyes of a soul
    we have known for many lives

Tiny particles collectively howling
a million stories carried in from worlds away

Some nights I cannot resist staying up
listening as the winds unravel
    our separateness.

The Earth My Body

Because the God I love lives inside of me
I must sometimes walk barefoot in the desert
and press my cheek against the hot dirt
to be closer to myself

Because my body is a petal
of this Earth
I can be fragile
as all love

Because I am rooted to these lands
I am strengthened under light of Sun
replenished under kiss of rain
illuminated under glow of moon

Because God is made whole through each life,
and each soul, including mine,
I know that if I keep praying
perhaps somewhere on this Earth
a sword will wilt

and maybe even a gun
will begin to shoot seeds
instead of bullets
and wide fields of sunflowers will bloom
where once there was war.

Milky Way

I am ripe flesh of stars desirous to shine
sweet cream of the Milky Way
within my lover's intertwine

I am a comet tail in the aurora
flashing trails of meteor showers
ancient secrets of the flowers of life
holding infinity inside of hours

I am daughter to seven sisters
who light a constellation
warm oils of sandlewood, cedar and myrrh
spun into libation

In human form I learned this much:
that all beings are made of light

and to that light we all return
To walk through the flames of fire
one must surrender to the burn

I am a moth who knows
each candle whispers my death
yet again and again I fly into the light
forsaking all the rest

I hear the voice of my ancestors
urging me to live each day as a precious gift
and the voice of my future children
singing great planetary shift

Redwoods, sequoia, sycamore and pine
reflections of the elders weighing on my mind
egret, eagle, hawk and fawn
the wise ones seem to rise with dawn

Six billion people made of dreams
a world crumbling at the seems
holocaust ripples and trails of tears
have we advanced much through the years?

Navy sonar interference, whales lost within the seas
satellite strewn skies and the vanishing of our bees

Orangutan, cheetah, Asian elephant and whopping crane
To the critically endangered species
may my prayers help ease your pain

I am a hieroglyphic portal
an Amazonian sacred vine
ripe flesh of stars ever desirous to shine

Shining across existence
burning across all time
scattered dust of the Milky Way
weaving comet tails into each rhyme

Ascension

In our loving we grew too enormous
to be caged inside four walls
so we gave away our belongings
set free on the whims of wind
slept under moons, rose with suns
bathed under the light of stars

Together we felt wilderness caressing our wildness
the spell of the sensuous descending upon us

The ancients sang to us the ways of beauty
and we grew strong as pieces of worlds fell apart,
rain forests were cleared, ice caps melted,
hearts were broken

And though the melancholy of the world could not be forgotten
we found love to be the most solid thing one could find

So we carried it with us down every secret trail
crouched reverently beside the trees
planted seeds and whispered *nourish them*

Across the vast ecstatic silence we felt the enormity
of our love spilling into everything
until it grew so big the whole Earth could not contain it

And we stood humble before each other,
sinking our feet into the soil
knowing nothing could stop our ascent towards the sky.

Shattering the Night

Many bodies will go to sleep lonely tonight
many hearts will yearn for someone to rise with,
And here and there, under the sheltering stars
scattered among the lonely,
true loves who have found each other
will whisper God's secrets into the night

There is one who holds us all, lovers and lonely alike,
through sandstorms and floods, feasts and famines,
genius and genesis

Across wide oceans I have sailed
piercing through gateways of the Orient,
spinning down ancient silk roads
always searching for this Great One

Galloping I have gone
swallowing up yesterdays, salivating for tomorrows,
carrying weary limbs across rolling pastures
of promised lands, a mighty and untamed mare
burning to be free

Many times I have shattered the night like a drunkard
naked on the ocean, praying for some holy touch of grace

And now, as one who has meandered
through dust and dreams
I have seen this much to know
the one I have searched for resides within

that diamond in the rough
who beats, throbs and breaks
in all far-reaching corners of the world
endlessly begging me to know truth.

Ojai Valley

I set out hiking into the twilight
as that swollen yellow-faced muse
rose from behind the mountain

The Chumash people had lived here once
and named this place Ojai, Valley of the Moon

Where were the Chumash now?

A few things we should never forget:

the ones who came before us
and the ways in which they lived
close to the Earth
in tribal community

close to the plants and animals
in daily reverence
keeping stories and hope alive
under stars and around fires

I vision quested alone that night
atop a moonlit mountain
listening to the wind
whisper again and again

Remember those who walked these lands before you.

I saw their faces. I heard their drumbeats.
I felt the spirit of their people breathing
through rock formations and stone creatures.
An owl stayed close by me all through the night

At daybreak I descended
finding my way back into town
where cars zipped to work, traffic lights flashed

and everywhere I turned I kept thinking
of the Chumash people
and this beloved land they called Ojai
Valley of the Moon.

Garden Spells

Woman in the mud of a fertile Earth
with the warmth of a hearth she tends the land
tender hands scoop dirt
offering each seed
with an unspoken prayer

Then dares to splay her legs atop the moonlit ground
spilling sounds of pleasure out to entice the nourishment to come

Come as it does
rich scent of garden mixed with sweat of skins
on nights like these one cannot tell
where one breath ends and the other begins.

Mama J

My Mother is a warrior
wearing the face of an ordinary woman
a beautiful woman no less
whose beauty I have marveled at
since my first breath
I carry her essence in the curls of my hair
her glow upon my cheeks
her joy inside my laughter

She has been a sliver of silver moonlight
lighting the way through challenging times
carrying me across triumphs and tragedies
on the soft wings of soothing words.

I was a little girl once and she used to sing
"Sunrise…Sunset… swiftly flow the days
seedlings turn overnight to sunflowers
blossoming even as we gaze"

Your only child is a grown woman
so very far from home
carrying our ancestors codes of light
deep inside my bones
DNA weaves our karma together
across the years
one season after another
through joyousness and tears

I don't remember growing up
but here I am forever young
Sunrise...Sunset...
remember when this song was sung?

My Mother, you are a warrior
with humble heart and beautiful face
I bow my head to my own life
and feel your benevolent grace

Sunrise...Sunset... swiftly go the days
sweet Mother of mine, though life is fleeting
I shall forever sing your praise.

The Small Stuff of Life

Life is so precious.
Every day brings us one step closer to leaving
this form we hold so dear
Why waste our time bickering over nothing
consumed by misunderstandings when the dolphins
are covered in oil and the rivers are drying up

It has been said not to sweat the small stuff, and most of it is
just small stufff. So why all this sweat and rage
this war and bloodshed when we could just fly

Why all this commotion over things that none of us
will ever take with us to that golden light we are destined for

To watch death come without warning for someone we love
is a reminder that this life is meant to be danced and celebrated
stale resentments meant to be forgiven
our beings meant to become great masters of compassion
forgiving instantly and holding onto nothing save love itself

For Revolution

These are the walls tumbling down
as our souls cry out for freedom
the sound of victory bells singing
with people who stand for what they know to be theirs.

These are the dreams woven into strands of DNA,
etched upon our skins, the flaming fires
of love and liberation that initiated us so long ago

These are the first cells that we were
to the miracle of brave sperm and egg from which we've
come

These are the endless ways we have bent our bodies
down twisting paths of dictatorship and repression,
genocide and incarceration, war and tyranny.

These are the red bloods that have been spilled
under the light of a golden sun,
who always knew through dawns and dusks
we were born to be free.

These are the prayers from kindred hearts like our own,
half a world away,

the dust of desert dwellers carried on the breeze,
the great destiny of an ancient civilization
where the wings of Isis first took flight.

This is the eye of Horus awakening between our eyes
the spell of blue lotus and hieroglyphic mysteries dripping
down temple doors, the wild songs of our soul
uttered in Arabic, Hebrew, Mandarin, Spanish, Swahili
and thousands of other tongues,

These are the songs
written inside the first cell of our destiny,
the inimitable cry of our souls to be free!

Voice of Water

I am the voice of water
liquid translator
of messages from the heart
of our galaxy
and galaxies beyond

Where I live life lives.

I am the tears and tides
rivers and rapids carrying
the codes and memories
of pristine worlds

I absorb your feelings
change according to your thoughts
and respond to the music around me

Drink with presence
and I shall bathe you from the inside out

I am meant to flow from
the mountain's source,
from headwaters of clear beauty
opaque clouds of rain and renewal

Do not let the sheer volume of ocean
on this Earth deceive you
I am sacred and I am scarce.

I am not to be squandered,
nor dumped into,
but prayed over.

Bless me and I shall bless you back.
Honor and protect me and I shall serve you
and seven generations to come.

I am liquid light. I am fluidity.
I am embodied love
flowing from the source
of Creation into every cell
of your being.

Drink from me with reverence
You have been thirsty too long.

Symphony of the Wind

All beings are made of music
I know this much is true

Animals in shackles, you are made of music too!
May captivity release its clenches, bells ring emancipation,
Songs of freedom remind us we are all of one great nation

Brothers and sisters caught in battle
for a moment do not shoot!
For the body of your enemy, like yours, is but a flute

May we harmonize together, tone in ancient ways
co-create a world where music spills across our days
May we carry soul and rhythm into each earnest endeavor
become oceans of melody that sing on into forever

We live in music. Music is who we are.
May we hear the ancient orchestras
emanating from the stars

Let us sense the Great Composer
working behind the scenes
and feel the force of rushing rivers carving steep ravines

The symphony of wind is singing tonight
mother moon is shining bright
and the great song we are prevails
across the all-pervading light.

Stillness

I know not about the strength to move mountains
but a few small things I have learned,

how to sit still upon them
how to climb their peaks and listen
to the crow's caw
how to be unmovable.

The Earth is quaking
and there is much talk about the next big one coming

Preparations are being made
provisions are being stored

All around me, these green mountains of stillness

These hummingbirds and butterflies
and the simple ways they go on
lighting up each day in beauty

They say the end is drawing near
but the wind is whispering
have no fear

Our molten Mother quakes and slides her plates
dealing us the hands of fate

It is her work to move the mountains
and ours, to find stillness
in the constant of such change.

A Midsummer Night's Dream

Once upon a starry night in a sultry land of steam
two lovers entwined in one another
entered a mid summer night's dream

That full moon was rising
constellations dripped with dew,
and water nymphs were busy casting spells
on all they knew

All the river's rapids were flowing
around them and within
as throbbing passion birthed a fire
flame had found its twin

Two souls had come together to share secrets through their
skin
as summer's song burned so strongly

~Sensuality could be no sin~

Bodies shook and quivered, molten gushing from their core
Twilight spilled into dawn and still their bodies throbbed for
more

A shooting star fell over them as Venus lit the sky
Oh Lover of Lovers you come to me with eternity in your
eye!

Rolling hills and valleys, all explosive mountain peak!
Oh Lover of Lovers within my depths,
you are the bounty that I reap!

And there in the jasmine gardens with sterling roses all abound
they poured the wine of divine intertwine
the most celestial of sounds
Moans and angel tones colored red
with passion's kiss, sweet breath of lovers laden
with the taste of honey bliss

A mid summer night so ripe and right,
transcending all the distance
love secrets spilling out across the lands
to fill this great existence

He turned to her and exclaimed,
Oh Lover pinch me if it's all a dream!
as the silent sun came
rising up across this sultry land of steam

They could not tell if they were dreaming or waking
as the veil was ever thin
though they felt the power of rushing rivers
all around them and within.

Riley

On the day you left your beautiful body
I placed some purple flowers between your paws
along with fresh mugwort, rosemary, and sage
the rest of the flowers I laid on an altar dedicated to you
Though they have been out of water this whole time
each bloom remains still fully alive and vibrantly purple

Two owls have seen serenading me each night
the stars seem to glow brighter than they ever have before

and I think death could be a great illusion
whose mystery unravels only once we have stared
into the heart of life itself

Your form I held so dear is gone
but in every direction I turn
our eternal love still blossoms

Running with the Wolves

Yes I am a woman who runs with the wolves
the coyote and the fox too
as well with all the small creatures and brave flowers
bursting out of the Earth with their faces towards the Sun

Really anyone and anything
who remind me to howl at the rising Moon
dance with the roaring wind
and live my days in wild abandon
from the depths of my untamed soul.

Two Souls

A flat red rock at the trail's end
took us in like two old friends
where we meditated together
soaring galaxies, becoming suns and moons
weaving through fertile worlds of untold beauty

He, a dog
and me, a human
and we, two souls alike
within and beyond the realms of Earthen fur and limbs
who wanted the same thing for ourselves

and the ants crawling atop the rock
and crickets chirping below
the gnarled roots of oaks
and ravens who call its branches home
the entire ecosystem of the forest
radiantly alive and humming
wanting the same thing for themselves as us
to love and to be loved

Isn't this what we all want before returning to dust?

Who would believe me if I said
my dog and I meditate together
and the red rock holds our prayers
and a butterfly sometimes lands on my dog's nose
and somewhere
in the forest of breathing souls
something simple and marvelous opens.

Lineage

What I remember most were his shoes
lone shoes he had worn for more than a dozen years
fastened together with layers of duct tape
and an unspoken pride for pennies saved

I remember at family gatherings
Gramps would insist everyone pass their plates down to him
and one by one he would lick them clean.

Before the war he was said to have been a brilliant writer
courting my Grandmother with romantic poetry
and an eloquent promise of bright tomorrows

When he returned, those closest to him became the pigeons
who he fed every day, rain or snow, for decades
He swam across the icy Charles River
on the harshest of Boston's winter days,
and read with a veracious appetite, books on many subjects
in many languages, all of which he had taught himself

Sometimes my Grandfather believed himself
to be the Messiah and would often announce himself
in that manner to visitors at the door

It was not until twenty years after his death
when I began to feel his uncanny madness for life
singing through me

And I began to see all the unconventionality in my own life
all the metaphorical icy rivers I had plunged myself into

all the owls, hawks, ravens and feathered friends I turned to
on my long walks in the woods

All the poetry, written in sudden blazes of early mornings
with a wild look in my eyes turning towards
the presence of some unseen Messiah

Who came sometimes through the verse
as if wanting me to tell the world,
It is alright to be different.

At the end of the day we have all gone a little crazy
trying to squeeze our boundless souls
into these tight human suits

And sometimes no matter how much duct tape
we wrap around these suits or how hard we attempt
to hold everything together
A wild spirit comes bursting out of the seems
with an insatiable appetite to lick the plates clean.

This was my Grandfather,
an occasional messiah in duct-taped shoes
who rose early each morning for his pigeon prayers
and stayed up late each night to write his poetry
just as I do now.

The Grace of Growth

These are no times for playing it safe
These are times for jumping into the river
For becoming learning trees ascending towards the Sun

These are times for our velvety prayers to billow out across Earth
for the cessation of all suffering

Times for drinking in the moonlight to feel her wisdom
rush into every mighty cell of our being

Times for knowing what constellations know.
For flowing like the rivers flow.
For glowing like the great light within glows.

These are times for the grace of small things
such as forgiveness and surrender

For random acts of compassion and kindness
For edible gardens to bloom in the middle of towns
For revolutions built on dancing and singing

These are times for communion and union with nature
for acknowledging the trees who shade this world
and the waters who give us life

Times for remembering our Mother
who we have pillaged, polluted, and poisoned
who still holds us,
who still nourishes us,
who still waits patiently for us to grow
And in her grace we do.

The Moon's Perspective

Once or twice love nearly destroyed me.

I swore to myself it was over
I would never love again

When I walked out
into the stillness of night
to consult with the moon about this
she told me that she too
had once been burned by love's woes
and had even been heart broken before

but nothing
she ever felt was worth fretting about
and nobody
she ever dared lose a good night's sleep over.

Worship

My church is the Earth and Sky
my temple the deep blue Ocean

Deer are my great gurus
Dolphins my high priests and priestesses

My reverends are the owls
who deliver nightly sermons
with such eloquence,
each morning I rise a better one

My holy scriptures are written
on the purple velvet blossoms of snap dragons
and the morning dew dripping from spider webs

I sing chorus with the frogs
bow down to the jungle vines

and kneel before the altar
of Mother Nature
where each ruby sunset
is as bold a miracle to behold
as walking on water

Full Moons are my messiah
Elephants my evangelists
and Dog is surely my God

Divine Reflection

You'd see them raising clenched fists,
stomping feet on midnight's street
clutching on to blame and shame,
a crying game in the name of love

Insane the ways a mind can melt
when heartfelt words are set ablaze
Now through a maze of streets they run
down moonlit alleys, up cobbled hills
where melancholy music spills

from window panes and frozen rains of silver tears
for yesteryear's unlaid dreams

The weather changes fast it seems.

Howling winds and impassioned fire,
desire burning through the freeze
then on the breeze a raven sang of pangs for every love forsaken
awakening them to dawn's perfection

~True love is our divine reflection~

In the aurora on a mountaintop
they stopped and turned to face each other
lover, best friend, teacher, muse

Choose the path of love always
and in every maze of cobbled streets
stomping feet and clenched up fists
one finds the grace of love persists.

Little Grasshopper

Patience little grasshopper,
all comes to pass in its right time
rewind, fast forward but all roads point
back to now.

Bow to the unseen Mystery
on the shores of surrender, so tender
a human heart who despite all that it resists
persists in the face of its true calling
falling in love...

Falling and rising and falling again
when are we fully healed?
Eyes revealed under the full moon's light
primal sight of lovers, whose scents cannot lie

Die 1000 times to be reborn
after each storm a rainbow

Worry not for the future nor dwell in the past
have patience little grasshopper
patience at last

Bosom Brigade

One day I would like to strip down in the woods
and stand naked before the loggers when they arrive

I would invite my sisters and sisters of their sisters
and every woman I know and don't know
to join me in silent vigil

And there in our dwindling forests and jungles
we would join hands to weave our curves
in figure 8s of protection around the trees

And as our nipples glistened in the sun,
our voluptuous backsides
would blind them with such beauty

And for a moment they would lay down their chainsaws
to watch us dancing under the green canopies

as radiant daughters of this Earth
who by way of the bosom brigade
refuse to let the mighty ones
who feed our lives and lungs be destroyed.

One day I would like to spread my legs
like the roots of a redwood tree
touching toes with all of my sisters
and sisters of their sisters
to birth to a new world order
where forests are holy ground
and chainsaws do not exist.

Wisdom from a Redwood Tree

Sink your roots into the Earth
Surround yourself with kindred spirits
Stand tall in the light
Be a pillar of strength and humility
Relish the silence
Keep rising through it all
Give thanks for the rainy days
Let yourself be hugged

Frog Croak

Live in the soul!
Live in the soul!
Live in the soul!

Listen to the frog croak rain soaked
wise old secrets in the mist,
to tender beats of hope and heartache
from every lover ever kissed

This great Earth keeps on spinning
These days keep rolling by
and sooner or later as fate would have it
each one of us must die

But the soul!
But the soul!
But the soul!
Its light that shall never diminish
Its beauty that knows no end
Burning on into infinity
Live in the soul I say my friend!

Listen to nightfall upon us
to the way love brings us to our knees
to spirits twining love divining
a light within that shall never cease

Live on the holy breath
Make your home in the sky and on sacred ground
Dance inside the naked song of love
Behold its eternal sound!

Stir the embers in the fire of your heart
Let all past pains heal and mend
Oh live in the soul and all truth shall unfold
In the soul!
In the soul my friend!

Love Heals

Thirty days at the most, the vet said somberly.
Silent rivers rushed down my cheeks
as I held him in my arms and burned
inside the fire that turns each one of us to ash.

Sometimes as he slept fitfully amidst strained breathing
I cried the silent tears of yesterdays gone by
I had to let go, and so I did,
but I never let go of hope

It's not that I was so terrified by death,
rather the idea of not offering the very best of myself
to this resplendent creature who had,
in every moment of our many years together,
offered the very best of himself to me.

In this life I had come to know some things
about about healing and wholeness, death and rebirth,
I had come to know about possibilities that exist
beyond what our eyes can see

And so I offered the best of myself to him
swirling tinctures and tonics, blessing his food with prayer
laying my hands down on him
with the all-penetrating light of love.

One day after several arduous months
he blew us away by running through the trails
like he was a puppy again. In circles he ran
with wagging tail and flopping ears,
jumping onto my lap like he had been reborn

Friends dashed over to behold the miracle
and every morning from then on,
he rose stronger and more inspiring to behold.

Now a year later he is perched in downward dog,
inhaling the familiar seductive scent of life,
with such zealous enthusiasm one could scarcely believe
how he rode death's edge.

Thirty days at the most the vet said somberly
as silent rivers fell down my cheeks.
Those rivers made an ocean
on which hope would come to float
and words like incurable and terminal
sank to the bottom of the ocean floor
as myself and all the dolphins sang aloud
for all the world to know
love heals
love truly heals.

Honeysuckle

The ripe sweetness of summer dripping from every sappy tree
and we, down on our knees in the sticky nectar of love
above, below, and all around, seem to have found
some hallowed kiss of grace
Your face in the moonlight my hidden treasure

One might measure wealth by savings in banks
but always give thanks for the golden days,
silver nights and emerald seas
and please remember to thank the bees

Honeysuckle of summer dripping from every hive
Reminding us true wealth resides in living fully alive.

To All Artists

All art in its myriad forms sings of God
and ultimately belongs to the Great Mystery

All we can do as artists is show up daily
with patience and humility

To be a channel of creation
receptive to any and all
lightning bolts of inspiration

If you are a dancer, dance!
If you are a writer, write!
If you are a musician, cast your songs
out to the witnessing moon!

Each baby step begets a leap of faith.
With nothing but a dream to grasp for
we go on creating,

tucked away in our little studios
with pen or paintbrush in hand
grasping the ungraspable
glimpsing the unglimpsable

To find the hand of God reaching out to meet us
beckoning us deeper and deeper
into the flickering gardens of creation.

To the Music Makers

To the music makers of this world singing for us to rise up
and remember the truth of who we are ~

To the ney player in Nubia,
the conga drummer in Cuba
the flamenco guitarist in Andalucia
strumming our passions through the night

To the Shipibo medicine woman curing with her rattle
To the Tibetan monk healing with his singing bowl
To the Hindu priest sounding his conch shell across the dawn
Awaken, awaken, awaken to the holy music that is this life!

To the ones composing cosmic choirs
to the ones serenading symphonies of wind
to the ones spinning naked beside orchestras of ocean

Devotion to the music makers of our world
who color our days with melody
who streak our nights with rhythm
who remind us that as above, so below

Let the music of our souls forever flow
Flow out freely to fill and spill into the hearts of one another
as we sing aloud:
Let the sweet, sweet music heal our Great Earth Mother!

Eagle Wisdom

Let your inner inkling precede all thinking
Build your life on the bones of the unknown
Follow your gut out of any rut
and remember,
we are never alone

Freshly fallen snow on a winter night
spring groves dancing with the aroma of citrus blossoms
firefly skies and sweet, salty oceans of summer
crisp foliage and the bountiful reaping of our harvest

If you are awake to it all
this is the greatest season of your life

www.ingramcontent.com/pod-product-compliance
Lightning Source LLC
LaVergne TN
LVHW091200080426
835509LV00006B/764